NATIONAL GEOGRAPHIC

Ladders

The
Sinking of the
Titanic

BUILDING T

In 1907, J. Bruce Ismay, managing director of the White Star Line, made big plans. He wanted to build a mammoth passenger ship. To do so, he collaborated with Lord William Pirie, the chairman of a shipbuilding company, and Thomas Andrews, an architect. The ship would be called *Titanic*.

And titanic she would be. *Titanic* would weigh more than 41,000 metric tons (46,000 tons), and measure 269 meters (294 yards) in length, about as long as three football fields placed end-to-end. She would be the largest passenger vessel in the world.

Ismay, Pirie, and Andrews wanted an unsinkable ship, and who wouldn't?

J. Bruce Ismay was managing director of the White Star Line.

Fig.4. SHELTER DECK. (G)

HE TITANIC

by Kathleen F. Lally

So the plans called for the body of the ship to be divided into 16 watertight compartments. The compartments were separated by thick steel doors. Even if four compartments were flooded, the air in the other compartments would keep *Titanic* afloat. That's because the **density,** or amount of matter in a compartment of air, is less than the density of that same compartment filled with water.

On March 31, 1909, workers laid *Titanic's* keel, or the spine of the ship. The rest of the ship would be built up from there.

Lord William Pirrie was a major shareholder of the White Star Line and chairman of Harland and Wolff shipbuilders.

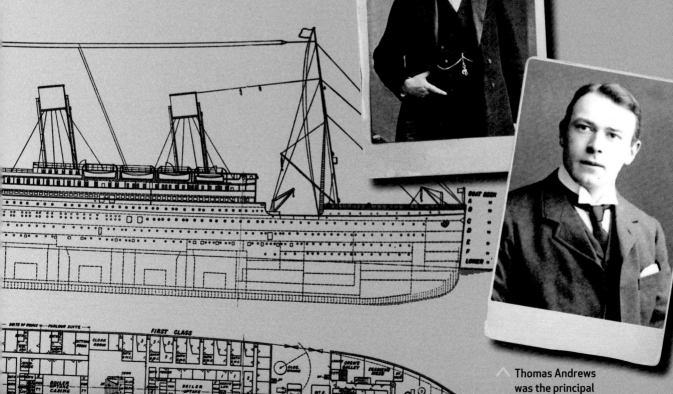

Thomas Andrews was the principal architect of *Titanic*.

3

FRAMING

At this point, the upper and lower parts of the stern, or back, of the ship are in position.

The fully framed bow, or front, of the ship shows the ship's size and shape.

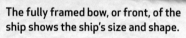

After laying the keel, workers began to frame *Titanic*'s hull or protective "shell." Workers installed girders on either side of the keel. Then they linked the girders by fixing steel bars across them.

Machines roared and hammers clanged as workers attached more than 600 framing ribs to the keel to form *Titanic*'s "skeleton." Like your ribs, framing ribs help give the ship its shape. More than 18 meters (20 yards) tall, the framing ribs were spaced at 1-meter (about 1-yard) intervals. Beams were attached to each frame by strong brackets. The finished framework was a super strong grid of interconnected boxes.

Next, workers attached steel plates to the hull framing in strips that overlapped. Picture a roof with overlapping shingles. The plates on *Titanic* overlapped in a similar way, but they were enormous! The largest of the steel plates measured 11 meters (12 yards) in length and weighed 37 metric tons (41 tons).

At the time, thick, stubby, nail-like rivets held together every steel structure. The bumps shown on the borders of these pages are the tops of rivets. Three million rivets, weighing about 11,000 metric tons (12,000 tons) all together, were used to build *Titanic*. Most of them were steel, and many were installed with huge riveting machines. Some sections of the ship did not have enough room to operate the riveting machines. There, workers had to hammer rivets in by hand.

To make the rivets easier to install by hand, workers used iron rivets instead of steel ones. The iron-making process at the time called for adding some ground-up slag, or waste rock, when the rivets were cast. Mixing in slag was tricky, however. A little slag can strengthen iron, but too much slag can make the rivets brittle, especially at low **temperatures.**

Inside floors begin to take shape.

The overlapping steel plates made the hull waterproof.

1910

FITTING OUT

With the framing and hull complete, *Titanic* was launched and moved to a deepwater wharf for the fitting-out process. Because of her great **mass,** or amount of material, it took five tugboats to haul her into the water! Fitting out included completing most of the remaining construction. It also included the installation of parts and equipment that were not built into the hull.

For the next ten months, *Titanic* went back and forth between the deepwater wharf and dry dock. A dry dock is a place on land where ships have work done and parts installed. Built especially for *Titanic*, the dry dock was the world's largest at the time.

Workers installed three gigantic propellers at the boat's rear: one on each side and one in the center. Behind the central propeller was *Titanic*'s rudder, which steered her. The rudder measured 24 meters (26 yards) high and 4.6 meters (5 yards) at its widest. Placed next to a seven-story building, the new rudder would have been taller!

Titanic was launched into the water stern first.

Work could be done on both the inside and outside of the *Titanic* when she was in dry dock.

Titanic's four smokestacks have yet to be installed.

1911

Huge propellers would drive the massive ship forward. Titanic needed enormous engines to power the propellers. Workers installed one engine for each propeller. The engines that drove the side propellers were each as big as a three-story house. For the center propeller, workers installed a smaller but more powerful engine. Huge, coal-fired boilers were installed to make steam to power the engines.

Early designs for Titanic included 64 lifeboats. Executives, however, objected that 64 lifeboats would clutter the Boat Deck. After all, why clutter the deck of an unsinkable ship with lifeboats? In the end, Titanic was equipped with only 20 rescue boats. They included 14 lifeboats that could each hold 65 people and two emergency boats that could each hold 40 people. They also included four collapsible boats that could each hold 47 people. The combined capacity was 1,178, enough for only about half of the over 2,200 passengers and crew who would sail on Titanic's first voyage. At the time, this was more lifeboats than the law required.

BON VOYAGE

Fitting out was nearly complete. Workers installed the major mechanical components of *Titanic* including three giant anchors. The main anchor weighed 16,000 kilograms (16 tons) and had 366 meters (400 yards) of chain. That is as long as four football fields end-to-end!

At the time, electricity was new technology and a big part of *Titanic's* attraction. So engineers designed four enormous steam-driven generators. They could generate more electricity than most land-based power stations of the day. *Titanic's* four giant funnels, or smokestacks, were hauled to the wharf. There, they were carefully installed on the uppermost Boat Deck. Carpenters, painters, and interior designers installed tiles, carpeting, and elegant furniture. Workers hung chandeliers and carted in expensive dishes and eating utensils.

The wife of the holder of this first-class ticket was ill. So he did not make the voyage.

Finally, *Titanic* was ready to sail. First she passed sailing tests to make sure she was seaworthy. Then, on the evening of April 2, 1912, *Titanic* left Belfast, Ireland, and arrived at Southampton, England on April 4. For the next six days, *Titanic* bustled with activity as the final touches were completed. The crew loaded enough food to last the journey. *Titanic's* crew of 913 men and women settled into their quarters.

By the morning of April 10, *Titanic* was ready for passengers to climb aboard. The stokers shoveled coal into the boilers. Just before noon, Captain Edward John Smith ordered the crew to depart from Southampton. Because the final destination of this first voyage was New York City, the American flag waved from the ship's mast. The crew and executives of White Star hoped *Titanic* would reach New York City in six days. With the blasts of two giant whistles and much fanfare, *Titanic* headed into open water.

Titanic begins inching her way out of Southampton on her maiden voyage.

Check In   During construction, which decisions might have led to the *Titanic* disaster?

The Night the *Titanic* Sank

edited by Barbara Keeler

TITANIC DISASTER GREAT LOSS OF LIFE

In *Titanic*'s day, newsboys staked out their favorite corners on which to sell newspapers. Here, newsboy Ned Parfett broadcasts the somber news outside the offices of the White Star Line in London the day after the disaster.

> ## "THE LOSS OF LIFE IN GREAT PART WAS DUE TO OVERCONFIDENCE, AS EVERY PERSON ON BOARD THOUGHT THE SHIP UNSINKABLE."

declared passenger C. E. Stengel of Newark, New Jersey. Stengel had just survived the sinking of the *Titanic*. Everyone had been wrong. *Titanic* was a sinkable ship after all.

Just before midnight on April 14, 1912, *Titanic* steamed through the North Atlantic, as two lookouts shivered in the frigid air of the crow's nest—a station high above the forward deck. They peered into the blackness ahead of them, on the lookout for enormous chunks of ice called icebergs. The **temperature** of the water was high enough that it was still liquid, but low enough that ice could stay solid. **Density** is the amount of matter in a certain volume. The density of solid water is less than the density of liquid water, which is the reason icebergs float. The ocean **current** had swept some of these icebergs toward *Titanic*.

Suddenly, Frederick Fleet, one of the lookouts, spotted something up ahead, looming huge and dark against the stars that dotted the night sky. He sprang into action—warning of the danger by ringing a bell three times and grabbing a telephone to call the bridge to report the ice. An officer immediately ordered that the engines be put in reverse . . . but it was too late.

As *Titanic* closed in on the iceberg, she slowly began to swing away, and scraped her side against the ice. Some rivets holding the hull together failed, which caused seams to open in the hull. Suddenly seawater rushed in to several forward compartments, nearly washing crew members off of their feet. Within minutes, frigid water whirled around their waists.

The air in the compartments was replaced with water, changing the overall density of the boat. It could not stay afloat for long.

Captain E. J. Smith ordered his crew to prepare the lifeboats. Because *Titanic* was thought to be unsinkable, it had only enough lifeboats for about half the people on board. Captain Smith knew not everyone would survive. Of more than 2,200 passengers and crew, only around 700 did. Some of them later told the tragic tale.

How many more people might have gotten in this lifeboat had they thought they would drown?

Caroline Bonnell

A FIRST-CLASS PASSENGER FROM YOUNGSTOWN, OHIO

"WELL, THANK GOODNESS, NATHALIE, WE ARE GOING TO SEE OUR ICEBERG AT LAST."

"That . . . was the one thing . . . that I said to my cousin as the great, beautiful *Titanic* was shivering beneath her death blow . . . at the very minute when the hand of death began pulling down its terrible cargo of souls.

"My cousin, Nathalie Wick, and I were . . . half asleep when the blow came. It was terrific. For a second the whole boat just stood stock still in its swift tracks and then it gave a great shiver all through.

"'Oh, she's hit an iceberg,' came ringing through the window in a woman's shrill voice. . . . Nathalie and I lay in bed and discussed whether or not we would get up to view the berg. . . . Finally we decided to 'go up' as we had been wanting to see an iceberg all the way over.

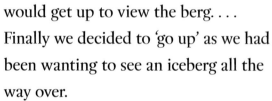

THE

VOL. XLIV—No. 309.

WITH BAND

ARCHIE B

TITANIC WEN

ALL UNCONSCIOUS OF PE
MEN KEPT PLAYING CARI
AFTER THE LINER STRUC

Beasley, of London Tells How Passenge
at First Refused to Believe Ship
Was Mortally Wounded—Res-
cue of the Lifeboats.

New York, April 18.—Follow

SOME PLAYING CARDS WHEN SHIP STRUCK

THE SHIP TAKES WATER INTO ITS HULL, AND PEOPLE ARE ORDERED INTO BOATS.

"The boat we were in was the first to strike the water. There were only twenty women, two sailors and a steward in it.

"After this the tragedy moved with a relentless swiftness . . . we watched the lights go out, as the boat dropped lower and lower into the sea. . . . Then the water rushed in . . . the orchestra played till the very last, and . . . the men went down into the sea singing 'Nearer, My God, To Thee.'

THE LIFEBOAT IS ROWED AWAY, LOOKING FOR RESCUE.

"The men became exhausted at the oars. So we women took a hand. And then . . . there was a big searchlight burning on the prow of a great liner. . . . It was that of the *Carpathia,* and we reached it in an hour.

"Women and men alike gave up their staterooms to us and slept on the floors of the library and smoking room.

"EVERYONE ON THE CARPATHIA WAS KINDNESS ITSELF."

ATLANTA, GA., FRIDAY MORNING, APRIL 19, 1912.—TWENTY-TWO PAGES.

PRICE, FIVE CENTS.

...AYING "NEARER MY GOD TO THEE

...FUTRELLE, ASTOR, STEAD, GUGGENHEIM ARE GONE

...TO OCEAN DEEPS WITH 1,595 SOULS

...THREE MISSING NOTABLES AND CARPATHIA

DECKS CROWDED WITH MEN WHO HAD ELECTED DEATH IN ORDER TO SAVE WOMEN

Women, Children and Few Men in the Lifeboats Saw the Great Ship Take Plunge Beneath the Icy Waves.

SHOTS HEARD ON SINKING...

F.D.MILLET   MAJOR BUTT

Thomas Whiteley

Warnings of Iceb
and Doomed Li

NATION HOLDING
AN INQUEST OVER
BODIES NOW LYING
AT BOTTOM OF SEA

Senate Committee Tear-

A WAITER ON THE *TITANIC*

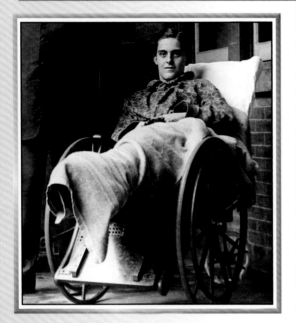

"I was awakened about 11:30 p.m. . . . a shipmate of mine said: 'No; we've hit a berg.'"

"I looked on deck and found it covered with ice. Stokehole No II began to fill with water at once.

"The order came 'All hands above decks with lifebelts.' The deck was crowded. The second officer was getting boat No. 1 ready. . . . I helped fill the boats. They were crowded with women and children.

"In some way I got overboard myself and found something to hold on to— an oak dresser about the size of this hospital bed.

"I WASN'T MORE THAN SIXTY FEET FROM THE *TITANIC* WHEN SHE WENT DOWN. I WAS AFT AND COULD SEE HER BIG STERN RISE UP IN AIR AS SHE WENT DOWN BOW FIRST."

"Then I drifted near a boat wrong side up. About thirty men were clinging to it. . . . I scrambled on to her. At 8:40 o'clock in the morning we were taken aboard the *Carpathia*."

RICHMOND, VA., SUNDAY, APRIL 21, 1912.   THE WEATHER TO-DAY—FAIR.   PRICE FIVE CENTS

s Ahead Allowed to Pass Unheeded,
Titanic Is Pushed On at Highest Speed

U. S. Senators Investigating Loss of Titanic

KNOWN FIVE HOURS
BEFORE COLLISION
OF VESSEL'S DANGER

Hearing Before Senate Committee Confirms
Fact That White Star Liner and All the
Lives She Bore Were Sacrificed That

Lawrence Beesley

A COLLEGE TEACHER TRAVELING IN SECOND CLASS

TITANIC HAS JUST HIT AN ICEBERG.

". . . there was no fear that the ship would sink. We were told by the officers that there was no danger.

> "WE WERE TOLD THAT THE *TITANIC* WAS UNSINKABLE AND THAT WE HAD NOTHING TO FEAR."

THE SHIP TAKES WATER INTO ITS HULL, AND PEOPLE ARE ORDERED INTO BOATS. BEASLEY BOARDS ONE.

"We were now about two miles from her, and all the crew insisted that such a tremendous wave would be formed by suction as she went down that we ought to get as far away as possible.

"She slowly tilted straight on end, with the stern vertically upward . . . we watched at least one hundred and fifty feet of the *Titanic* towering up above the level of the sea and looming black against the sky. Then with a quiet slanting dive she disappeared beneath the waters. . . ."

Other Voices

MRS. WILLIAM BUCKNELL

"The greater portion of the first cabin passengers gathered in the main saloon after the crash, but as the general belief was that the ship was unsinkable some of the women returned to their cabins and retired."

ROBERT W. DANIEL

"After waiting for an interminable time with the collapsible boat in my hands, I felt the *Titanic* sinking under my feet . . . I tried to wait, but suddenly found myself leaping from the rail, away up in the air, and it felt an eternity before I hit the water. When I came up I felt that I was being drawn in by the suction, and when I felt a cake of ice near I clung to it."

JOHAN CERVIN SVENSSON, AGE 14

" . . . My mother told me when I kissed her goodby in Sweden that if anything happened to run to the lifeboats and that's what I did."

TO REACH SURVIVORS IN TIME, *CARPATHIA* HAD TO SPEED THROUGH ICE FIELDS.

SIR HENRY ARTHUR ROSTRON, CAPTAIN OF *CARPATHIA*

"And it is a great wonder to me that we ourselves didn't split on one of them— those most treacherous, most deadly enemies of those who go down to the sea in ships."

> Captain Rostron's account of *Carpathia's* response

The Modern Historic Records Association

RMS "Carpathia"
Cunard SS Co. Ltd.
At Sea
April 27th 1912.

At 12.35 am (ship's time) April 15th (Monday) 1912, I was called by the 1st officer in company with marconi operator & informed that the White Star Line R.m.S. "Titanic" was sending out urgent distress signals by wireless, that she had struck ice & required immediate assistance also giving position of "Titanic" as Lat 41°46' N. Long 50°14' W.

I immediately ordered the "Carpathia" turned round, sent for the Chief Engineer, made out course & found we were then S52°E (true, 58 miles from "Titanic" also sent wireless to "Titanic" saying we were coming to his assistance. The "Carpathia" was then on a voyage from New York to Mediterranean ports, with passengers, mail & cargo.

I gave Chief Engineer instructions to throw out another watch of stokers & to make all speed possible.

I then ordered all our boats prepared & swung out ready for lowering. Interviewed the head officials of each department giving them all instructions I considered necessary to meet any emergency & then I . . .

18

ANSWERS IN HINDSIGHT

After the disaster, some passengers and crew pointed out that more lives may have been saved if safety been assigned a greater priority. Today's experts agree. If better decisions had been made during construction, even more lives might have been saved. For example, if steel rivets had been used instead of iron rivets, would seams have opened up in the hull? Nobody knows. Metal becomes more brittle at freezing temperatures. Iron is more brittle than steel, and too much slag mixed in can make iron even more brittle. In 1997, Commander Brian Penoyer, a specialist in investigating marine disasters, asked metal experts to examine rivets recovered from the wreckage. These rivets contained enough slag to make them brittle at freezing temperatures.

The original plan of 64 lifeboats could have saved all the passengers and crew. Plus, if the 20 rescue boats on *Titanic* had been filled to capacity, nearly 500 more people could have been saved.

Advancements in technology mean that ships today are less likely to sink. New methods of producing steel make it more durable and less brittle than during the early 1900s. Today's steel ships are usually welded together rather than riveted. Plus, they have more lifeboats than *Titanic* had.

Check In How were the physical properties of *Titanic* changed after she hit the iceberg?

Alvin

by Judy Elgin Jensen

the Submersible

As eager as people were to find *Titanic*, it was impossible at the time she sank. Engineers had not developed the tools or technology to descend as deep as *Titanic* lay. *Titanic* would not be found until years later, after new technologies enabled engineers to design underwater equipment that could withstand the tremendous pressures of the water in the deepest parts of the ocean.

With advancements in technology, finding *Titanic* became possible. Engineers designed vehicles that could carry scientists to great ocean depths. These submersibles, or submarine-like vehicles, can operate underwater in frigid temperatures and under enormous pressure.

One such submersible was *Alvin*. Built in 1964, it was once owned by the U.S. Navy. In it, two scientists and a pilot could explore the deep ocean waters and almost two-thirds of the ocean floor. They could maneuver the submersible as deep as 4.5 kilometers (3 miles) for up to ten hours.

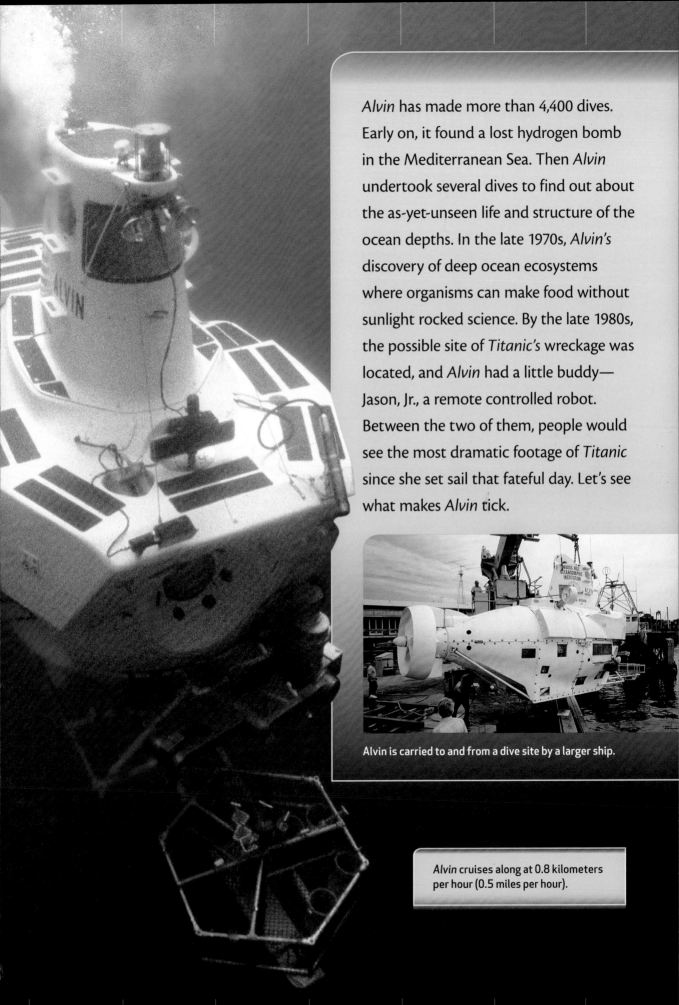

Alvin has made more than 4,400 dives. Early on, it found a lost hydrogen bomb in the Mediterranean Sea. Then *Alvin* undertook several dives to find out about the as-yet-unseen life and structure of the ocean depths. In the late 1970s, *Alvin's* discovery of deep ocean ecosystems where organisms can make food without sunlight rocked science. By the late 1980s, the possible site of *Titanic's* wreckage was located, and *Alvin* had a little buddy—Jason, Jr., a remote controlled robot. Between the two of them, people would see the most dramatic footage of *Titanic* since she set sail that fateful day. Let's see what makes *Alvin* tick.

Alvin is carried to and from a dive site by a larger ship.

Alvin cruises along at 0.8 kilometers per hour (0.5 miles per hour).

Alvin's Technology

To design *Alvin*, engineers first looked at nature's problems they had to solve. How does a bubble of metal sink to great depths with the pull of **gravity,** and then be **buoyant** enough to float back to the surface against gravity's pull? How can we keep that bubble from being crushed at great depths? What about keeping the explorers warm in near-freezing water?

Then engineers thought about what the explorers would need in a submersible— the ability to sink, rise, move in all directions, and sometimes to just hover.

Alvin also needed special equipment to allow researchers to do their work. Cameras, recorders, robotic arms, measuring devices, sampling kits— *Alvin* needed to have it all.

Fiberglass and foam cover *Alvin* and protect the controls, electronics, and batteries. *Alvin's* cockpit walls are about 5 centimeters (2 inches) thick.

The propeller allows the pilot to steer *Alvin* in different directions.

Alvin has tanks with water and air. The pilot adjusts the amount of water and air in the tanks to change *Alvin's* **density.**

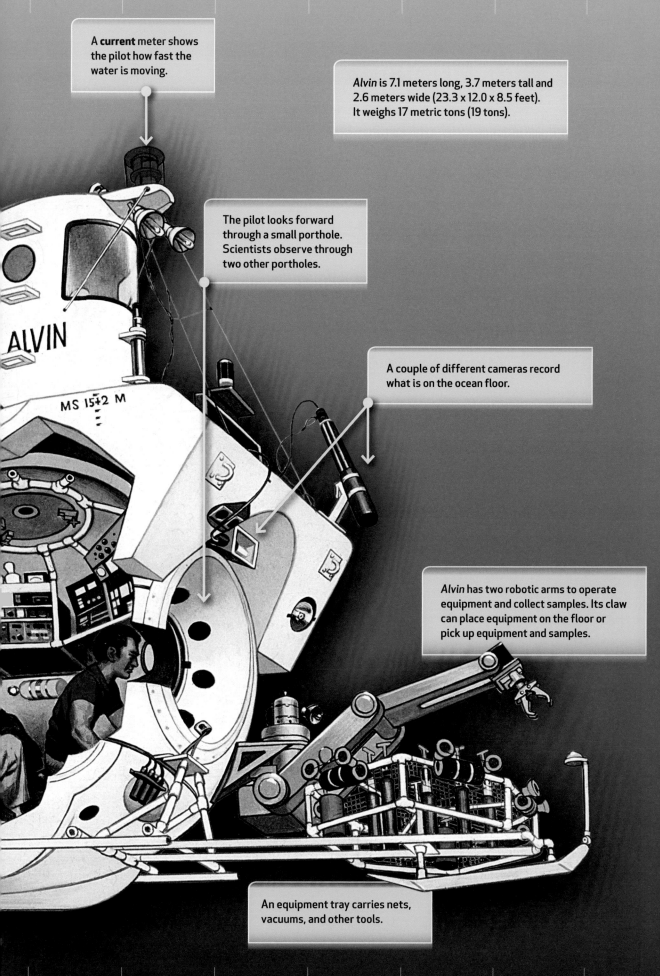

A **current** meter shows the pilot how fast the water is moving.

Alvin is 7.1 meters long, 3.7 meters tall and 2.6 meters wide (23.3 x 12.0 x 8.5 feet). It weighs 17 metric tons (19 tons).

The pilot looks forward through a small porthole. Scientists observe through two other portholes.

A couple of different cameras record what is on the ocean floor.

Alvin has two robotic arms to operate equipment and collect samples. Its claw can place equipment on the floor or pick up equipment and samples.

ALVIN

MS 15+2 M

An equipment tray carries nets, vacuums, and other tools.

Alvin Finds Titanic

For 73 years, *Titanic* rested undiscovered on the dark depths of the ocean floor over 3 kilometers (2 miles) below the surface. People were eager to find the wreckage. At first, it was impossible. In fact, even the ship's exact location was a mystery. Then on September 1, 1985, a team led by oceanographer Robert Ballard used *Alvin* to search the ocean floor. From historical records, they knew roughly where *Titanic* went down. Using advanced imaging technology, the dive ship that carried *Alvin* located a huge field of debris on the ocean floor.

Alvin's sonar, a device that uses sound to locate large objects under water, stopped working. The team needed a navigator aboard the dive ship to guide them to the site of the wreckage.

Just as Ballard's team was about to ascend, the ocean floor began to slope up suddenly into a mound of mud. *Alvin* slowly moved forward until researchers saw a vast expanse of black steel rising out of the bottom. *Titanic* was inches away! Because of *Alvin's* equipment problems, however, the explorers ascended immediately. But, THEY HAD FOUND IT!

Alvin was repaired aboard the dive ship. In the days that followed, the team made a series of dives. They saw *Titanic's* enormous steel plates crumbling in rust. Her woodwork had been devoured by wood-boring organisms. They had left hollow calcium tubes behind. Ballard later wrote, "On one dive, as we moved in slow motion along the hull, the darkened portholes seemed to me like rows of sightless eyes brimming with great tears of rust."

The bow and the stern were widely separated. The bow was in much better shape than the stern, which was in pieces. The team found some clues to how the ice had damaged *Titanic's* hull. "As we moved slowly along that vertical wall of steel, I half-expected to see a tear in the plates," wrote Ballard later. "But there was nothing—only an indication that the plates had bent inward and the rivets holding them together perhaps had sprung, allowing seawater to enter."

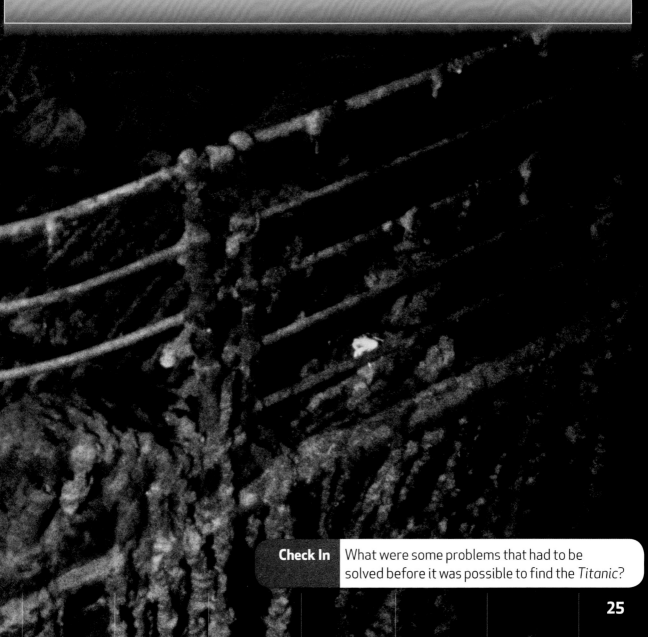

Check In What were some problems that had to be solved before it was possible to find the *Titanic*?

TITANIC ARTIFACTS

by Barbara Keeler

Imagine your first glimpse of shoes, combs, hand mirrors, dishes, iron benches, light fixtures, silver coins, small electric heaters, the head of a doll, unopened bottles of beverages, a large steamer trunk, a deck chair frame, and a statue of the goddess Diana scattered about the ocean floor. What would you do?

Once neatly stacked in *Titanic*'s kitchen, these dishes would have been used in the first-class dining room above.

When Robert Ballard discovered the wreck of *Titanic* in 1985, he saw thousands of artifacts on the ship and strewn across the ocean floor. His action? He photographed them. Ballard's team didn't remove anything from the wreckage—not even a few coins from the bag of a ship's officer that also contained keys, watches, and jewelry. According to the laws of the sea, removing anything would have meant that Ballard and his team owned the site. If they had, nobody else would be allowed to remove anything.

Two years after *Titanic's* discovery, a private company removed artifacts and—guess what? In doing so, the company claimed the wreck for itself! RMS Titanic, Inc. began salvaging the ship's artifacts for exhibition. Since then, the company has conducted seven research expeditions to the wreck. It has recovered more than 5,500 artifacts from the sea floor.

RMS Titanic, Inc. holds exhibitions around the country. For the price of admission, people can see such items as a chef's hat, a razor, lumps of coal, serving dishes, shoes, bottles of perfume, a leather bag, clothing, letters, plumbing pieces, portholes, and an unopened champagne bottle. Studded with rivets and ribbed with steel, a gigantic slab of *Titanic's* hull is on display, too—all 13.6 metric tons (15 tons) of it!

Tourists flock to view *Titanic's* salvaged artifacts on display. They even buy tiny pieces of coal from the ship as keepsakes. Many people agree with RMS Titanic, Inc. that *Titanic's* artifacts should be on display for the world to see. After all, more than 25 million exhibition visitors can't be wrong!

While tourists could hire a submersible to take them to the bottom of the ocean to explore the wreckage site, that's an expensive destination where few can travel. Representatives of RMS Titanic, Inc. argue that the company offers an important service by making the history and artifacts of *Titanic* widely available.

Since millions have paid to view the exhibits, it is clear that the general public is very curious about the disaster. Additionally, some family members of the passengers and crew are interested in retrieving objects from the deep water.

Without the salvage team to bring family heirlooms to the surface, these items and the memories they bring would be lost to the sea forever. RMS Titanic, Inc. maintains that its mission is to recover the artifacts because the ship is rapidly deteriorating on the ocean floor. They cite scientists' estimates that the wreck will eventually collapse and be destroyed. Over time, water has corroded, or broken down, metal parts of the ship.

Adding to the concern about chemical deterioration is a new species of **bacteria**, or tiny organisms. The bacteria have been discovered on the sunken hull of *Titanic*. By eating away the wood and metal, they may be speeding up the decay of the wreck, new research reports.

Another argument for salvaging is that bringing up parts of *Titanic* have helped explain why the ship sank. For example, investigators analyzed *Titanic's* rivets. The investigation revealed that they contained materials that could have made them brittle and more likely to crack. Perhaps figuring out more about what happened may help prevent future disasters.

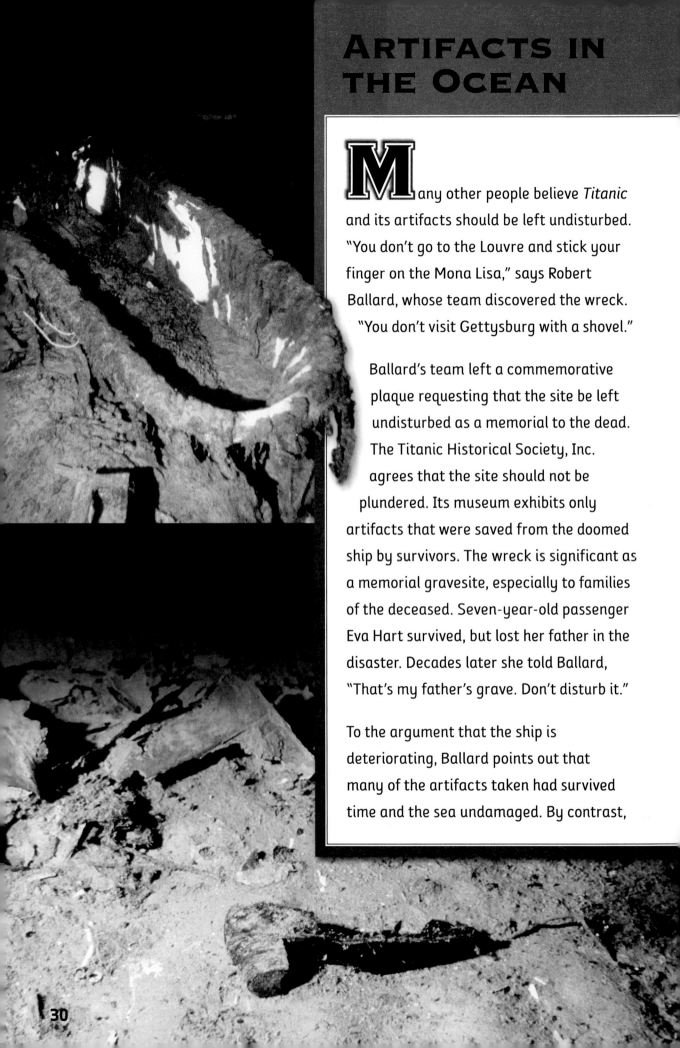

ARTIFACTS IN THE OCEAN

Many other people believe *Titanic* and its artifacts should be left undisturbed. "You don't go to the Louvre and stick your finger on the Mona Lisa," says Robert Ballard, whose team discovered the wreck. "You don't visit Gettysburg with a shovel."

Ballard's team left a commemorative plaque requesting that the site be left undisturbed as a memorial to the dead. The Titanic Historical Society, Inc. agrees that the site should not be plundered. Its museum exhibits only artifacts that were saved from the doomed ship by survivors. The wreck is significant as a memorial gravesite, especially to families of the deceased. Seven-year-old passenger Eva Hart survived, but lost her father in the disaster. Decades later she told Ballard, "That's my father's grave. Don't disturb it."

To the argument that the ship is deteriorating, Ballard points out that many of the artifacts taken had survived time and the sea undamaged. By contrast,

Titanic itself has been damaged by salvagers, according to Ballard. "The mainmast of the ship has been bashed down and destroyed. Objects—the ship's bell, the ship's light—have been torn off," he said. Large areas of the deck have been damaged, he adds.

Another problem is litter. Many ships that transport submarines to carry tourists to the underwater site have dumped debris into the ocean and onto *Titanic*. The submersibles themselves have left their dive weights on or near *Titanic*. The problem may go beyond the litter itself. One expert is concerned that dumped trash may be feeding bacteria that are eating away at the ship.

Ballard prefers making *Titanic* widely accessible through technology such as video cameras. Everyone with a television set or digital device could enjoy *Titanic* and see it better than they could from a submersible's porthole. A remote viewing experience would be better and more complete if the wreck and its artifacts are left undisturbed. "The place is just as important as an object from the place," Ballard says.

Check In What do you think should be done with artifacts from *Titanic*? Use statements from Ballard and RMS Titanic, Inc. to support your opinion.

Discuss

1. How did the information in "Building the *Titanic*" supply you with background information for the other three pieces in the book?

2. Based on the information in "Building the *Titanic*" and "The Night the *Titanic* Sank," cite two pieces of evidence that you think were the biggest reasons for loss of life.

3. Use examples from "*Alvin* the Submersible" to explain how engineers considered physical properties of materials when building *Alvin*.

4. Both *Alvin* and *Titanic* could sink and float. How does the concept of density relate to this statement?

5. After reading "*Titanic's* Artifacts," what more information would you need in order to decide if artifacts should be retrieved? How could you find the information?